GW01086567

WHAT WOULD IT TAKE TO BUILD A

TIME MACHINE?

BY YVETTE LaPIERRE

raintree
a Capstone company — publishers for children

Raintree is an imprint of Capstone Global Library Limited, a company incorporated in England and Wales having its registered office at 264 Banbury Road, Oxford, OX2 7DY – Registered company number: 6695582

www.raintree.co.uk
myorders@raintree.co.uk

Edited by Arnold Ringstad
Designed by Laura Graphenteen
Original illustrations © Capstone Global Library Limited 2021
Originated by Capstone Global Library Ltd
Printed and bound in India

978 1 4747 9347 6 (hardback)
978 1 4747 9688 0 (paperback)

British Library Cataloguing in Publication Data
A full catalogue record for this book is available from the British Library.

Acknowledgements
We would like to thank the following for permission to reproduce photographs: Alamy: Richard Watkins, 25; Getty Images: Dursun Aydemir / Anadolu Agency, 18–19, Timothy A. Clary / AFP, 27; iStockphoto: RichVintage, 29; NASA: JSC, 8; Shutterstock Images: 3000ad, 22, andrey_l, 24, Anton Chernigovskii, 9, Esteban De Armas, cover, Gorodenkoff, 4, Hallowedland, 12, Interior Design, 15, iurii, 10–11, muratart, 6, oorka, 16, Xristoforov, 5; SpaceX: 21
Design Elements: Shutterstock Images

Every effort has been made to contact copyright holders of material reproduced in this book. Any omissions will be rectified in subsequent printings if notice is given to the publisher.

All the internet addresses (URLs) given in this book were valid at the time of going to press. However, due to the dynamic nature of the internet, some addresses may have changed, or sites may have changed or ceased to exist since publication. While the author and publisher regret any inconvenience this may cause readers, no responsibility for any such changes can be accepted by either the author or the publisher.

CONTENTS

CHAPTER ONE
A JOURNEY THROUGH TIME........ 4

CHAPTER TWO
WHAT IS A TIME MACHINE?........ 7

CHAPTER THREE
HOW WOULD A TIME MACHINE WORK?........ 8

CHAPTER FOUR
CURRENT TECH........ 17

CHAPTER FIVE
WHAT TECH IS NEEDED?........ 20

CHAPTER SIX
WHAT COULD THE FUTURE LOOK LIKE?........ 25

GLOSSARY........ 30
FIND OUT MORE........ 31
INDEX........ 32

WORDS IN BOLD ARE IN THE GLOSSARY.

A JOURNEY THROUGH TIME

There is a loud noise and a flash of light in an ancient forest. Dinosaurs look up from their leafy dinner. They see the dust settling around a strange, shiny object. Suddenly a door opens and a person steps out. The person is wearing modern clothes. It's a time traveller!

A time traveller stepping out into an ancient world is common in stories.

The time machine from *Back to the Future* became one of the most famous film time machines.

People have dreamed of time travel for years. Time travel has appeared in books and films for a long time. H. G. Wells wrote *The Time Machine* in 1895. The book's hero goes to the future. The *Back to the Future* films started in 1985. Characters in these stories travel in time. *Avengers: Endgame* was a huge hit in 2019. Its story included time travel.

The idea of time travel may seem unreal. But scientists believe it may be possible.

Planes travel in three dimensions. Time machines would travel in a fourth dimension: time.

CHAPTER TWO

WHAT IS A TIME MACHINE?

Any time traveller must first understand what time is. Scientists consider time a fourth **dimension**. We can see three dimensions in the space around us. Cars travel through two dimensions. They drive forwards and backwards. They steer from side to side. Planes travel through a third dimension. They fly up and down in the air. Time is a fourth dimension. Together, space and time make up space-time. A time machine is a vehicle that travels through space-time.

Films sometimes show time machines as objects on Earth. A person steps into the machine. They close the door. Then they travel through time. This is not how scientists think real time machines might work. Instead, a time machine would probably need to be a spaceship.

CHAPTER THREE

HOW WOULD A TIME MACHINE WORK?

Scientists have some ideas about how time travel could work. Usually these ideas have to do with strange things that happen in space. High speeds can have unusual effects. So can strange things in space called **black holes**. And some objects in space may let us zoom from one place and time to another. For these ways of time travel, the time machine is just a spaceship.

Putting on a spacesuit could be the first step in time travel.

Strange things found in space may make time travel possible.

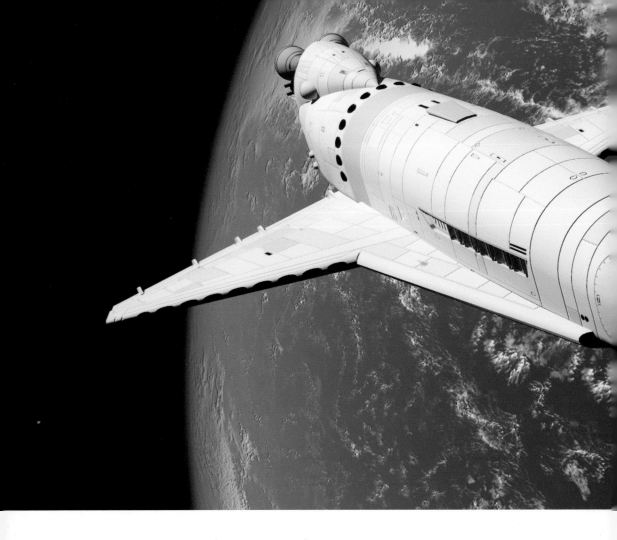

What is the fastest speed you can go? Scientists believe going faster than light is impossible. Light moves at 299,792 kilometres (186,282 miles) per second. This is much faster than cars, planes or even today's spaceships. But in the future, new spaceships with very powerful engines could be built. They may allow astronauts to zoom through space at nearly the speed of light. What happens at these high speeds?

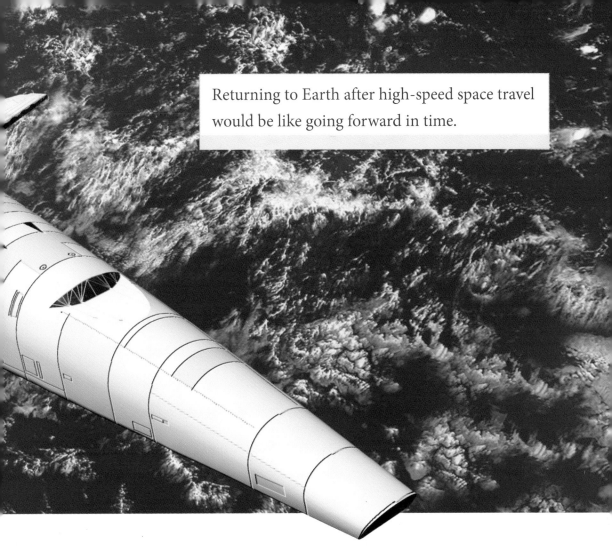

Returning to Earth after high-speed space travel would be like going forward in time.

When you move close to the speed of light, time slows down for you. Imagine you are in a spaceship. You leave Earth and travel at these high speeds for one day. Then you return to Earth. On Earth, one year might have passed. But to you, only one day passed. You have travelled forward in time.

Scientists still have much to learn about black holes.

Black holes could be another way to move through time. Black holes form when large stars burn out. They are areas with very high **gravity**. They draw in everything nearby. Dust, gas and even light swirl into the black hole. Once something gets sucked in, it cannot escape.

Scientists believe that high gravity can slow down time. The higher the gravity, the slower time moves. A spaceship could get close to a black hole. It would stay far enough away to not get sucked in. But it would feel the strong gravity. Time would slow down for the people on board. When they returned to Earth, they would have travelled forward in time.

BLACK HOLE DANGERS

Scientists believe getting too close to a black hole would be deadly. Once a person is close, the gravity would pull at them. It would pull more strongly at the parts closer to the black hole. This means it would stretch the person. Scientists compare this to being turned into spaghetti.

A third way to time travel would be using a **wormhole**. A wormhole is a tunnel through space-time. Space-time has wrinkles in it. Scientists think wormholes might form in the wrinkles. A wormhole leads from one place and time to another. It works like a shortcut.

Imagine space-time is a sheet of paper with two dots on it. You want to go from one dot to the other. Normally you must travel across the sheet. But what if the sheet were folded so the dots touched? Then you could move directly between the dots. This is how a wormhole might work. A spaceship would enter a wormhole at one point. It would leave at another. It might end up in another time.

TRAVELLING WITH A WORMHOLE

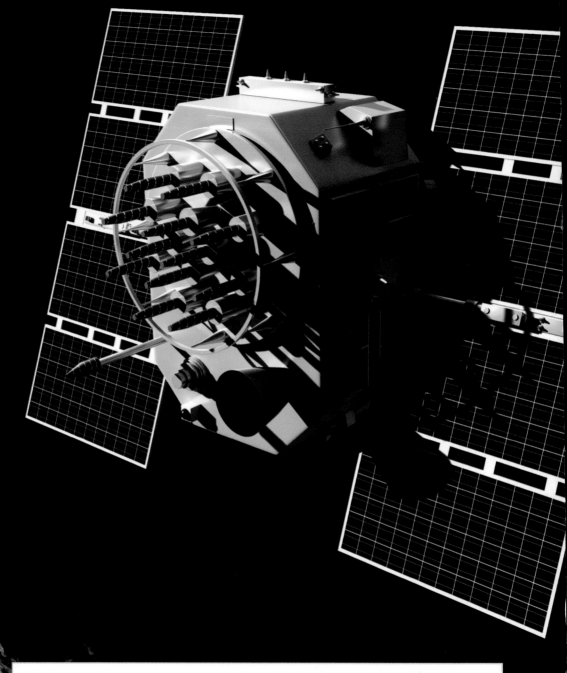

GPS satellites are about 20,200 kilometres (12,550 miles) above Earth.

CHAPTER FOUR

CURRENT TECH

Time machines are a long way from being invented. Some of the science behind time travel is well known. But other parts are just guesses at the moment.

Scientists already know that travelling fast slows down time. They must plan for how this affects **Global Positioning System** (GPS) satellites. These spacecraft circle Earth. They send signals to devices on the ground. A device receives the signals. Then the device can work out its own exact location. GPS relies on careful timing. The satellites are moving so fast that their clocks run a bit faster than normal. Scientists had to correct for this difference to make GPS work.

FUN FACT

More than 30 GPS satellites are in space today.

Scientists also know a lot about black holes. They have studied black holes for many years. No one has been close to a black hole. Scientists study them through telescopes. Scientists have seen the gas and dust swirling into them. In April 2019, they took the first-ever photos of a black hole itself.

Scientists showed and talked about the first-ever photo of a black hole at an event in 2019.

The science behind wormholes is less clear. Scientists think they may exist. But they have never seen one. And some scientists think that even if wormholes do exist, people could not survive journeys through them.

CHAPTER FIVE

WHAT TECH IS NEEDED?

Spaceships must get better to make time travel possible. Today's spaceships go very fast. But they do not go nearly fast enough. The fastest speed ever reached by humans was on the Apollo 10 mission in 1969. The astronauts travelled at 39,897 kilometres (24,791 miles) per hour on their way back from the Moon. The speed of light is about 27,000 times faster than that. Spaceships would need faster engines to reach such high speeds.

Spaceships would also need powerful engines to travel to black holes. Black holes are very far away. It would take today's ships many thousands of years to get to a black hole. Ships would need to get much faster.

Today's rockets are powerful enough to blast spaceships into space. But reaching light speed would take even better technology.

Spaceships will need technology that hasn't been invented yet to fly into a wormhole.

The ships would also need to be very strong. Strong gravity could damage ships. It could even rip weak ships apart. The ships would need good computers too. These computers would have to steer ships close to a black hole, but not too close.

Wormholes have special challenges. If they exist, they may be tiny. Or they may exist for just a moment and then quickly disappear. Special machines may be needed to make a wormhole larger and hold it open. Other machines may even allow people to build their own wormholes. Scientists do not know what these technologies might look like. If wormhole time travel ever happens, it will probably be in the far future.

FUN FACT

An Austrian scientist called Ludwig Flamm was the first scientist to say that wormholes might exist. He described wormholes in 1916.

No one truly knows what time travel might be like.

CHAPTER SIX

WHAT COULD THE FUTURE LOOK LIKE?

Time travel may be a long way off. Scientists still have much to learn. But thinking about time travel can be fun. This is why time travel is so popular in stories. People think about the adventures they could have in time. The more scientists learn, the closer we may get to a real time machine.

In the *Back to the Future* films, the time machine is a silver sports car.

What could you do with forward time travel? You could zoom forwards a few months to enjoy a new film you are looking forward to seeing. You could travel many years ahead to see the future. Maybe you want to see how the world will change.

What could you do with backward time travel? Perhaps you could use it for research. You could go back in time to see a dinosaur. You could see important events.

Some museum displays make people feel like they are walking with dinosaurs. A time machine could make a scene like this real!

Time travel isn't possible today. Scientists are continuing to study how it might work. If scientists built a time machine, would you climb aboard? Where would you go if you could travel in time?

TIME TRAVEL PROBLEMS

Thinking about time travel can quickly become confusing. Imagine if a person travelled back in time. She might do something that could change history. What if she stopped her parents from meeting? Does that mean she was never born?

Would you suit up for a trip through space and time?

GLOSSARY

black hole area in space with very strong gravity

dimension measure in one direction, such as length, depth and height

Global Positioning System electronic tool that receives signals from satellites in the sky to find the location of objects on Earth

gravity force that pulls objects together; gravity pulls objects towards things such as Earth or black holes

wormhole tunnel through space-time

FIND OUT MORE

BOOKS

Exploring Black Holes and Other Space Mysteries (Science of the Future), Tom Jackson (Raintree, 2020)

Gravity (Great Scientific Theories), Nick Hunter (Raintree, 2017)

Space: A Children's Encyclopedia, DK (DK Children, 2010)

Universe (DKfindout!), DK (DK, Children, 2018)

WEBSITES

www.bbc.co.uk/bitesize/topics/zx339j6/articles/zy3g7p3
Find out more about how to write a science fiction story.

www.esa.int/kids/en/learn/Our_Universe/Story_of_the_Universe/Black_Holes
Find out more about black holes.

INDEX

Apollo 10 mission 20
Avengers: Endgame 5

Back to the Future 5
black holes 8, 12–13, 18, 20, 22

dimensions 7
dinosaurs 4, 26

Flamm, Ludwig 23

Global Positioning System (GPS) 17

light speed 10–11, 20

spaceships 7, 8, 10–11, 13, 14, 20, 22
space-time 7, 14, 15

Time Machine, The 5

Wells, H. G. 5
wormholes 14, 15, 19, 23